OXFORD BOOKWORMS LIBRARY

Human Interest

The Children of the New Forest

Stage 2 (700 headwords)

Series Editor: Jennifer Bassett
Founder Editor: Tricia Hedge
Activities Editors: Jennifer Bassett and Alison Baxter

THE CHILDREN
OF THE NEW FOREST

It is 1647 and the four Beverley children – Edward, Humphrey, Alice, and little Edith – are in hiding in the New Forest. The King of England is in prison, and there is fighting everywhere in the country – Cromwell's men against the King's men. And if you are a friend of the King, you are in great danger.

The children's father died while fighting for the King, their mother is dead, Cromwell's soldiers have burnt their home, and they have no money, no food, nothing. But they have one true friend – old Jacob Armitage. So now, with Jacob to help them, they must learn to live off the land – to hunt for meat in the forest, to plant vegetables, to look after the pigs and chickens.

But Cromwell's men are everywhere, and the children must learn never to say that their name is Beverley . . .

CAPTAIN MARRYAT

The Children
of the New Forest

Retold by
Rowena Akinyemi

OXFORD UNIVERSITY PRESS

OXFORD
UNIVERSITY PRESS

Great Clarendon Street, Oxford OX2 6DP

Oxford University Press is a department of the University of Oxford.
It furthers the University's objective of excellence in research, scholarship,
and education by publishing worldwide in

Oxford New York

Auckland Cape Town Dar es Salaam Hong Kong Karachi
Kuala Lumpur Madrid Melbourne Mexico City Nairobi
New Delhi Shanghai Taipei Toronto

With offices in

Argentina Austria Brazil Chile Czech Republic France Greece
Guatemala Hungary Italy Japan Poland Portugal Singapore
South Korea Switzerland Thailand Turkey Ukraine Vietnam

OXFORD and OXFORD ENGLISH are registered trade marks of
Oxford University Press in the UK and in certain other countries

ISBN 978 0 19 479054 3

A complete recording of this Bookworms edition of
The Children of the New Forest is available on audio CD ISBN 978 0 19 478977 6

Printed in China

ACKNOWLEDGEMENTS
Illustrated by: Alan Marks

Word count (main text): 6,605 words

For more information on the Oxford Bookworms Library,
visit www.oup.com/bookworms

CONTENTS

1

Escape!

One day in November 1647, Jacob Armitage hurried through the New Forest to the house of Arnwood.

'You must leave this house immediately,' he said to Edward Beverley. 'Come with me to pack your things. You must come to my home and stay there.'

'But why, Jacob?' Edward asked the old man. 'Why?'

'The King has escaped from his prison at Hampton Court,' Jacob explained. 'He's riding south through the forest, and Cromwell's soldiers are searching for him. And I've just heard a group of soldiers in the forest –

'The King has escaped from Hampton Court.'

they were talking about Arnwood. They know that your father was the King's friend, and they're planning to burn Arnwood tonight, because they think the King is hiding here.'

'Burn Arnwood! They can't do that! It's *my* house, and I'm staying here!' Edward said angrily. He was fourteen years old, the oldest of the four Beverley children.

The Beverley children lived alone at Arnwood, with an old woman who did the cooking and all the work of the house. Their father, Colonel Beverley, was killed while fighting for King Charles I at Naseby in 1645. Before he left home, he asked Jacob, a poor forester who lived near Arnwood, to look after his family. Jacob knew the family well and was happy to do this. And when the children's mother died a few months later, Jacob came every day to visit the children and to help them.

'My dear boy,' Jacob said, 'remember your sisters and brother. The soldiers will shoot them, or burn them in the house. No, no, you must all come with me.'

In the end, Edward agreed. He and his brother Humphrey, who was twelve, packed their things. Then they put them on Jacob's horse, White Billy, who was waiting outside.

Jacob told Alice, who was eleven, and Edith, who was eight, that they were going to visit his home in the forest. He did not tell them about the soldiers.

'Edward, here is my key,' said Jacob quietly. 'Lock the door of the house, and take my gun from the wall. Don't leave your brother and sisters. I'll help the cook to pack her things, and then I'll follow you.'

The four children left the big house and went into the forest with White Billy. It was five o'clock in the afternoon, and already dark. Jacob helped the cook, who hurried away to her family in Lymington, and then he hid in the trees near the house, and waited.

After a while he heard horses, and the Parliamentary soldiers arrived. Soon they were in the gardens and all round the house. A few minutes later Jacob saw black smoke going up into the sky; then he saw flames at the windows. Arnwood was burning!

Then Jacob saw flames at the windows.
Arnwood was burning!

3

'It is done,' thought Jacob, and he hurried away into the forest. In half an hour he arrived at his cottage. He looked back and saw the flames of Arnwood shooting higher and higher above the trees.

When he knocked on his door, Edward opened it and came out with Smoker, Jacob's big dog.

'My sisters are asleep in bed,' Edward told Jacob. Then Edward saw the flames of Arnwood and the angry red light between the trees, and he was silent.

'I told you,' Jacob said. 'The soldiers didn't look for you in the house before they burnt it.'

'Arnwood is *my* house!' said Edward angrily. 'And when I'm a man, I'll fight Cromwell's soldiers for this!'

'Perhaps you will,' Jacob said quietly. 'But let's go inside now. It's a cold night.'

Edward slowly followed Jacob into the cottage. He hated Cromwell and the Parliamentary soldiers. First they killed his father, and now they burnt his house. He lay down on the bed, but he did not sleep.

Jacob lived alone because his wife was dead, and he had no children. His cottage had one large room for living and cooking, and three small bedrooms behind. Outside there were a few chickens and pigs in one field and some old fruit trees in another field.

The next morning Jacob began to teach the children

*Outside the cottage there were a few
chickens and pigs in a field.*

how to cook and to clean the cottage. It was all new
work to them, because rich children like the Beverleys
never cooked or worked in the house.

'You must stay inside today,' Jacob told them, 'because
the soldiers are still searching the forest. Let's get some

dinner ready. We can all help. Edward, will you go and get some water from the river?'

The children enjoyed cooking their first meal. They washed some potatoes and cut some meat and vegetables into pieces. Then they put them with some water in a pot on the fire. Little Edith put plates and knives on the table.

While the dinner was cooking, Edward stood outside the cottage, watching out for soldiers, and the other three made the cottage tidy. But just before dinner was ready, Edward ran back inside.

'I can see soldiers, and they're riding this way!'

Jacob was silent for a minute. 'My dear children, those soldiers will search the cottage, and I don't want them to

The children enjoyed cooking their first meal.

6

see your rich clothes. You must go to bed and pretend to be ill. Edward, you can put on one of my old shirts.'

The younger children got into bed and hid their rich clothes. Edward put on Jacob's old shirt and sat next to the bed with a cup of water for his sisters. Quickly, Jacob put away the plates and knives. Soon there was a knock on the door.

'Come in,' said Jacob.

'Who are you, my friend?' asked one of the soldiers.

'A poor forester, sir,' replied Jacob, 'in great trouble. My grandchildren are all in bed, very ill.'

'We must search your cottage for the King.'

'Very well – but please don't frighten the children.'

The men began to search the cottage. Edith screamed when she saw them, but Edward told her not to be afraid.

'There's nothing here,' one of the soldiers said. 'Let's go. I'm tired and hungry.'

'There's something here that smells good,' said another soldier. 'What is it?' he asked, looking into the pot.

'My dinner for a week,' explained Jacob. 'I can't light a fire every day, so I cook once a week.'

'Well, it looks good, so we'll try some,' the soldiers said. And they put the pot on the table, sat down, and ate everything. Then they thanked Jacob and rode away.

Jacob called the children and told them to get up. 'The soldiers have gone,' he said.

Edith screamed when she saw the soldiers.

'And our dinners have gone too,' said Humphrey, looking at the dirty plates and the empty pot.

'Bad men ate our dinner,' said Edith.

'We can cook another,' said Jacob. 'We're all hungry, but if everyone helps, the dinner will soon be ready.'

After dinner, Jacob told the children that their lives must change. 'The King's enemies think that you are dead, burned in Arnwood. But you are still in danger, and so you must stay here with me and pretend to be my grandchildren. You are children of the New Forest now.'

2

Life in the Forest

The next morning Jacob rode to the town of Lymington. There he heard that the King was in prison again and that Cromwell's soldiers were going back to London. Jacob bought cottage clothes for the children and a few things for the house. Then he put everything on his horse and walked back home through the forest.

While he walked, he thought about the children. They were so young, and alone in a dangerous world – he was their only friend. But he was an old man, and perhaps would not live long. He knew he must teach them how to find food and do everything for themselves.

After dinner, he called the children round him. 'Now, remember, you are my grandchildren and your name is Armitage, not Beverley. I've bought you some cottage clothes to wear, and you must all learn to work and live like a forester's children. Edward is the oldest and he must come out with me into the forest and learn how to hunt. Then we'll have meat to eat every day. Humphrey, you must look after the horse and the pigs, and bring water from the river every day. Alice dear, you must light the fire, clean the house and wash the clothes, and you and Humphrey will both learn how to cook. And little

Edith will look after the chickens and look for the eggs every morning – will you, Edith?'

'Yes,' said Edith. 'I liked the chickens at Arnwood.'

There was no more meat in the cottage and so the next morning Jacob and Edward, with the dog Smoker, went out into the forest. They walked quietly and did not speak. The red deer of the forest could see, hear and smell very well, and it was hard to get near them.

After more than a mile, Jacob dropped down to the ground, and through the trees Edward saw three deer. Jacob moved silently forward on his hands and knees, and Edward and Smoker followed him. Slowly they got nearer, but then suddenly the deer, who were quietly eating grass, put up their heads and walked away.

Jacob turned. 'You see, Edward, hunting is slow work. Now we must go through the woods around the other side of the deer and try again.'

'What frightened them, do you think?' asked Edward.

'When you were following me, I think you put your knee on a piece of stick and it broke.'

'Yes, but that made only a little noise.'

'Only a little noise will frighten a red deer,' said Jacob kindly. 'But these mistakes can happen to anyone, and you will learn. Now – not a word, and not a sound!'

In half an hour they found the deer again, and again Jacob dropped down to the ground and moved forward without a sound. At last, he lifted his gun and shot one of the deer behind the shoulder. The deer dropped to its knees and fell dead, and the other deer ran away.

'This is a fine deer and the meat will be good,' said Jacob. 'We're about five miles from the cottage, Edward, but Smoker will take you home, and you can come back

Suddenly the deer put up their heads and walked away.

with White Billy. He must carry the meat home for us.'

It was a good beginning to their new life, and the next day Jacob rode to Lymington to sell some of the meat. With the money he bought things for the vegetable garden, a big bag of oatmeal for the winter, and a gun for Edward.

That winter was long and cold, and they stayed in the cottage most of the time. Alice learned how to cook and to mend clothes. Edith learned to read and write, and to make oatmeal bread and cook it on the stones by the fire. Humphrey was clever with his hands, and learned how to make things out of wood. Edward learned how to shoot and to look after his gun. They were all busy and happy, but Edward sometimes felt angry. He kept his father's sword by his bed and often cleaned it. He hated Cromwell and his soldiers, and he wanted to fight for the King.

Edward kept his father's sword by his bed and often cleaned it.

12

In the month of May, the leaves came out and the forest began to look green again. 'And now, Edward,' said Jacob one day, 'we need more meat, both to eat and to sell. So let's get our guns and go out. You can shoot first.'

They walked four or five miles before they saw a deer. 'Stay here, while I go through the trees with Smoker,' said Jacob quietly. 'Then I'll stand up, and the deer will run towards you. Remember, shoot it behind the shoulder.'

Edward waited quietly, and after a time the deer ran out of the trees in front of him. He lifted his gun, shot the deer behind the shoulder, and it fell to the ground.

'Well done!' said Jacob, when he came back. 'You killed your first deer! And it's a fine one, too. Soon I shall leave the hunting to you, and put my gun up on the wall!'

The spring was a busy time for everyone at the cottage. In the field they planted potatoes and lots of different vegetables. Little Edith was busy with her chickens, and Humphrey built a chicken-house, and a house for the pigs. Jacob sold some of the deer meat and bought a little cart. White Billy was not very happy about this at first, but he soon learned to pull the cart behind him, and it was a great help with all the farm work.

Humphrey loved the work on the farm. He was always making plans to do new things, and he was now very clever at building things out of wood. It was hard work. First he had to cut down a tree, and then cut the wood

13

The spring was a busy time for everyone at the cottage.

into pieces for building. One day he began to build a cow-house.

'We need a cow to give us milk,' he said to the others. 'I'm going to catch one of the forest cows.'

Edward laughed, but Jacob said, 'The forest cows are very wild, and can be dangerous. You must be careful.'

June arrived, and they began to cut the long grass, to keep for food for the animals in winter. The girls helped too, and White Billy was busy every day, pulling home the new cart full of summer grass.

Humphrey did not forget about his cow. He finished building the cow-house and began to spend an hour or more every day out in the forest. He was watching the wild cows. Early one morning he came running home.

'Jacob, Edward, come with me! Bring Smoker, too.'

'Why, what's the matter?'

'I've found a cow! She's left the other cows because of her new-born calf. So she's alone, and we can catch her.'

'But how?' asked Edward.

'I'll tell you later. I must get White Billy and the cart.' Jacob and Edward followed him, and soon they were driving the cart through the forest.

'Smoker will jump up at the cow,' explained Humphrey, 'and keep her away from us while we put the calf in the cart. When we drive away, the cow will follow her baby.'

15

The cow was lying near her calf, but when she saw them, she got up and shook her head angrily from side to side.

'Go, Smoker, go!' Jacob called to his dog, and Smoker jumped at the cow, driving her back into the trees away from her calf. Edward and Humphrey quickly lifted the calf into the cart, and got in themselves.

Then Jacob hurried back and got in too. 'Drive off, Humphrey,' he said. 'I'll call Smoker now, and the cow will follow us. Here, Smoker, here!'

Smoker came running out of the trees at once. The cow followed and ran wildly after the cart, calling loudly to her calf. Before long they were back at the cottage.

The cow followed and ran wildly after the cart.

'There's Alice and Edith running out!' cried Jacob. 'Go back inside, Alice! The cow is dangerous!'

Humphrey drove the cart into the field. Smoker kept the cow away while they carried the calf into the cowhouse. Then they left, and the cow followed its calf inside.

'There!' said Humphrey. 'Let's leave her with the calf. Tomorrow I'll cut some grass for her.'

Every day for a fortnight Humphrey brought grass to the cow, and every day she was a little quieter. After a month, Humphrey began to take milk from the cow.

'I have learned how to shoot deer,' said Edward. 'But Humphrey has caught a cow and given us milk. You are cleverer than I am, brother!'

3

Edward goes visiting

And so the summer went by, and every day was busier than the one before. Humphrey caught two more calves, and they now had more pigs and chickens. Jacob took some of the new young chickens to Lymington to sell, and bought salt and oatmeal, pots for the kitchen, and a gun for Humphrey.

King Charles was still in prison, and Cromwell's men went on killing their enemies and stealing the houses and land of the King's friends. Edward could not forget that he was a Beverley of Arnwood, and was often angry.

'I want to be a soldier like our father,' he told Humphrey. 'I want to fight for the King, and tell the world that my name is Beverley!'

'If you do that, Cromwell's men will put you in prison,' Humphrey said. 'I know how you feel, Edward, but for now you must stay here with us. What will happen to our sisters if you leave? I can't do all the work, and poor Jacob is getting old and tired.'

It was true. Jacob was nearly seventy-six years old and no longer strong. That winter he was often ill and could not leave the cottage. Edward did most of the hunting. He was now very good at it, and knew the forest well.

Early in 1649 Humphrey told Jacob that he needed another dog. 'Smoker is a hunting dog,' he said. 'I need a dog to help me with all the farm animals.'

'A puppy will learn most easily,' said Jacob. 'Oswald Partridge, a forester who lives on the other side of the forest, always has puppies, and he will give us one. But Edward, you must go. I cannot ride that far. Tell Oswald that you are my grandson. He'll be a good friend to you. But remember, your name is Armitage!'

'A puppy will learn most easily.'

The next morning Edward rode White Billy across the forest. He was happy to go out into the world again, but he knew he must be careful. After two hours he arrived at some cottages and knocked on the first door. A girl aged about fourteen opened the door, and told him that Oswald Partridge was out in the forest.

'I must wait for him, then,' said Edward. 'I've come to ask him for a puppy for my grandfather, Jacob Armitage.'

'Wait a minute,' the girl said. She went inside, and then came back. 'You must come and speak to my father.'

Edward followed the girl inside. The man sitting at a table was dressed like one of Cromwell's men. His tall hat lay on a chair with his sword underneath it. The girl sat down by the fire, and the man went on reading a letter. He did not look at Edward for two or three minutes.

Edward felt angry. But he was just a poor, unimportant forester, he remembered. So he said nothing, and waited.

'What's your business, young man?' the man said at last.

'I came, sir, to see Oswald Partridge about a puppy for my grandfather, Jacob Armitage.'

'Armitage!' The man looked at some papers on the table. 'Yes, one of the foresters. Why hasn't he visited me?'

'Why must he see you, sir?'

'Because Cromwell has given the New Forest to me, to look after for Parliament. My name is Hetherstone, and all the foresters now work for me.'

'My grandfather has not heard this, sir,' said Edward. 'The New Forest belongs to the King, and my grandfather is one of the King's foresters. But he has a cottage and a

'What's your business, young man?' said the man at last.

farm which belong to him, and not the King.'

'Yes, I know about Jacob Armitage. And I know that he was Colonel Beverley's friend. The Colonel was a brave man, it's true, but he fought for the King and so was an enemy of Parliament. Tell me, were you a friend of the Beverley family?'

'When I was a child, I lived at Arnwood with the Beverley children.'

'And where were you when the soldiers burned Arnwood?'

'I was at my grandfather's cottage,' replied Edward, his eyes wild with anger.

'I can understand why you feel angry about that.' Mr Hetherstone shook his head slowly. 'Those soldiers did a terrible, terrible thing,' he said quietly. Then he looked up at Edward again. 'But you must understand, young man, that your grandfather can no longer work as a forester. I cannot give work to people who are friends of the King. The forest deer now belong to Cromwell, and if you shoot any deer, you will go to prison for it.'

'Sir,' Edward said quietly, 'the King himself is in prison and so he cannot pay his foresters. If they kill the deer, it is because they must have food to eat. I am sure the King will understand that his people must live.'

'Well, well, those are brave words. But you will still go to prison if we catch you. Now, you can go to the kitchen and wait for Oswald.' Mr Hetherstone turned to his daughter. 'Patience, give Armitage something to eat.'

Edward went out and took White Billy to the stables behind the cottage, then followed Patience to the kitchen. 'I came here for a puppy,' he thought, 'and I have found a Roundhead – who sends a Beverley of Arnwood to eat in the kitchen! But he is sorry about the burning of Arnwood, so I don't hate him.'

Edward saw that Patience was a beautiful girl.

Patience put food on the table. Edward thanked her and sat down to eat. Patience smiled, and Edward saw that she was a beautiful girl.

Later, he met Oswald Partridge and saw his dogs. Oswald was very surprised to see him. 'I never knew Jacob had a grandson,' he said. 'I never knew he had a son! Are you on the King's side, like Jacob?'

'To the death,' replied Edward, 'when the time comes.'

'Ah, then you can have one of my puppies,' Oswald said. He told Edward a bit about Mr Hetherstone. 'He's one of Cromwell's good friends, they say, but he's not a bad man. There are much worse than him. I've kept my job, but many haven't. We must all be careful these days.'

It was now late, so Edward stayed the night in a room above the stables. There was no bed and no door, and Edward could not sleep because he was so cold. Soon he got up and began to walk around outside, to get warm.

There was a light upstairs at one of the windows of the Hetherstones' cottage, which was strangely bright. Edward watched it. He saw someone moving in the room, and suddenly he saw flames. The room was burning!

'Fire! Fire!' he shouted. He ran back to the stables and found a ladder. Then he quickly climbed up it to the window, broke the glass, and got into the room. There was smoke everywhere, and he fell over a body on the floor. Quickly, he lifted the body and moved back to the window. The flames were now running along the floor, getting higher and higher. With the body in his arms, he got out on to the ladder, but the flames caught his shirt, burning his arm. He climbed down and carried the body into the stables. There he saw that it was Patience Hetherstone.

Edward ran outside again, and saw that other people were coming with buckets of water. There was a lot of shouting, and Edward was soon up the ladder again while others carried buckets of water up to him.

In the crowd below, Mr Hetherstone was trying to get near the ladder. 'Save her!' he cried. 'My daughter's up there! She'll burn to death!'

At the top of the ladder, Edward did not hear his cries, but a voice came from the crowd: 'There were four burned at Arnwood.'

'My daughter's up there!' cried Mr Hetherstone.
'She'll burn to death!'

Mr Hetherstone fell down, his face white, and some men carried him into another cottage.

At last the fire was put out, and Edward came down the ladder. He called Oswald and they went to the stables. Patience was still lying on the floor, but her eyes were now open. She was alive!

They gave her some water and carried her to Oswald's cottage. Then Edward said quietly to Oswald, 'I shall ride home now at once. Come and visit Jacob soon if you can. He's not been well all this winter.'

'But Mr Hetherstone will want to thank you for saving his daughter's life,' said Oswald.

'I don't want Mr Hetherstone's thanks. I want nothing from the King's enemy,' said Edward. He rode home with Humphrey's puppy inside his coat. His arm was badly burned, and it was a long time before it was better.

4

Secretary to Mr Hetherstone

When Edward arrived back at the cottage, Humphrey came out to meet him, and his face was unhappy.

'Oh Edward, Jacob is very ill. The girls are with him now. We think he's dying.'

Edward hurried inside, and the four children stayed

by Jacob's bedside all that day. In the evening Jacob spoke to them all very lovingly, one by one. Those were his last words, and a little later, he died.

The children cried for a long time because they dearly loved the good old man. The next morning they buried him under an oak tree behind the cottage, and they planted wild flowers above his body.

They buried Jacob under an oak tree behind the cottage.

'We have lost a good friend,' said Edward. 'He saved us from the flames of Arnwood and he has looked after us since then in his cottage. We must now look after ourselves, and try to be happy together.'

Six weeks went by, and then Oswald Partridge came to visit them. 'How is the old man?' was his first question.

'We buried him six weeks ago,' replied Edward.

'I'm sorry to hear it,' said the forester. 'He was a good man. And how is your arm?'

'Nearly well,' said Edward. 'Now, sit down, Oswald. Tell me, why didn't you visit us sooner?'

'In a word – murder. These terrible Roundheads have killed the King. A few days after the fire, Mr Hetherstone went to London. He told me to stay near his cottage to look after his daughter. In London he tried to stop the murder, but Cromwell and his men didn't listen to him. He came home yesterday, and told us all about it.'

'The King murdered!' cried Edward. 'How can they murder a King? Well, the time will come. If I cannot fight for the King, one day I shall fight against his murderers.'

Oswald stayed to eat dinner at the cottage, and was very friendly with them all. He stayed the night and the next day Edward decided to tell him their secret.

'Colonel Beverley's children?' said Oswald. 'Well, this is happy news! And it's true, Edward, that you don't look like a forester's son. Mr Hetherstone thinks that

'How can they murder a king?' cried Edward.

too. He has asked me lots of questions about you, and he says that he will visit you himself to thank you for saving his daughter's life. But I'll keep your secret, and I shall be happy to help the Colonel's children.'

'Then can you tell me how much to pay for oatmeal and salt?' said Edward. 'And who will buy deer meat and pay well for it? You see,' he went on, 'now that Jacob is dead, I must go to Lymington myself to do these things.'

Oswald told him the names of men who would buy deer meat – and ask no questions. 'But be careful, Edward. Mr Hetherstone would like to help you because you saved his daughter's life, but he cannot save you from the soldiers if they catch you killing the forest deer.'

During that summer Edward and Humphrey went hunting together when they needed meat. They kept a careful watch for strangers, but they knew the forest well now and could move as silently and as cleverly as the deer. Humphrey's farm was getting bigger all the time. With the vegetable gardens, and the chickens and cows and pigs, it was hard work for them all, but the children never went hungry – thanks to Jacob Armitage's teaching.

One day Humphrey was out in the forest, getting food for the pigs, and he found a Spanish gipsy boy lying on the ground. The boy was nearly dead from hunger and thirst, and Humphrey carried him back to the cottage.

One day Humphrey found a Spanish gipsy boy
lying on the ground.

Alice and Edith looked after him, and when he was well again, they asked him to stay and work on the farm.

The boy's name was Pablo and he was about fifteen years old. His English was not very good, and he had no friends, no family. He was happy to stay at the cottage.

'Lost in the forest. No food, no water. Nearly dead,' he explained. 'You save my life. Happy to work for you. Happy to have food and bed. Happy to have new friends.'

It was nearly winter when Mr Hetherstone, with his daughter Patience, came to the cottage. At first Alice and Edith were afraid when they saw his tall hat, but he spoke kindly to them all. And Patience took Edward's hand and thanked him again and again for saving her life.

Then Mr Hetherstone spoke to Edward. 'You saved my only child from the fire, Edward Armitage, and I thank you.'

'Mr Hetherstone, I cannot understand you,' Edward said. 'You are a good man – but you are a friend of Cromwell, who has murdered the King!'

'Edward, you are young and you can't remember the troubles in England because of King Charles. He never listened to Parliament, he did only what he wanted, and the people were very angry. They fought because they wanted to be free. But now Cromwell and his friends will listen to nobody. They have murdered the King, and

31

'We shall all be friends,' said Patience when they said goodbye.

they are worse than he ever was. One day the people of England will be free again. But for now we can't speak of these things openly – it's too dangerous.'

'Thank you, sir,' said Edward quietly. 'I understand

you better now. I'll try to be careful, because I want to fight against Cromwell when the time is right.'

Mr Hetherstone looked kindly at Edward. 'Now, I want to help you. You know that you were born for better things than a forester's life. I would like you to be my secretary and live at my house. I will pay you and you can help your family. Don't answer me now. Talk to your brother about it first.'

Alice and Edith made dinner, and they all ate together. Patience enjoyed the farm very much, and she liked Alice and Edith. 'We shall all be friends,' she said when they said goodbye. And she smiled her beautiful smile.

Later, Edward talked to Humphrey. 'What shall I do? I want to be a soldier, not a secretary,' he said.

'You're too young,' said Humphrey. 'I like working on the farm, and now I have Pablo to help me. I know that you want to get out into the world, but for now you must take this job. Mr Hetherstone will be a good friend to us all.'

So Edward bought a black suit and a tall hat, kissed his sisters goodbye, and went to live in Mr Hetherstone's cottage. Every morning he wrote letters for Mr Hetherstone, and every afternoon he spent time with his daughter. He began to like Patience very much. Every week he rode across the forest to see his family. Sometimes Patience went with him, to visit Alice and Edith.

And so a year and more went by. The next winter there was a lot of snow and travelling was difficult. But in the world outside, things were happening, and news came to Mr Hetherstone in the spring.

'The King's son has arrived in Scotland and is now King Charles II,' he told Edward. 'He's coming south with his army to England, and I think the time is right for you to ride north and meet him. I'll give you letters to some friends who will help you.'

And so the next morning Edward said goodbye to Patience and kissed her hand. She cried to see him go. Then, with his father's sword by his side, Edward rode away on Mr Hetherstone's black horse, to fight for the King at last.

5
Soldier of the King

Edward had many adventures. He made new friends, and the King was very pleased to learn that the children of Colonel Beverley were alive and well. But the time was not yet right for King Charles II. Cromwell's army was still very strong, and by autumn 1651 the King's soldiers were either dead, or running away, back to Scotland. The King himself escaped alone – no one knew where.

Edward returned secretly to the New Forest, wearing the uniform of a dead Roundhead soldier. He arrived at the cottage late at night and frightened his family and Pablo very much. Then they heard his voice, and in a minute Edward was in the arms of his brother and sisters.

Early the next morning Edward rode across the forest to see Mr Hetherstone, who was very pleased to see him. He listened to Edward's news, then said:

'So, we must wait a while longer before we see a new King, and we must still pretend to be Cromwell's friends. We'll say that you went to fight for Cromwell. It was

In a minute Edward was in the arms of his brother and sisters.

clever of you to come back in a Roundhead's uniform – that will help to keep both of us out of danger.'

For some days Cromwell's men searched the forest for the King. Then came news that the King was now in France, and at last the soldiers left the forest.

Edward returned to his job of secretary to Mr Hetherstone. Patience was very pleased to see him again, but Edward felt uncomfortable. He now wanted to tell Patience that he loved her, and he wanted to tell her father the secret of his name. But he was still a young man, and he did not know how to do either of these things.

One evening he found himself alone in the garden with Patience. For a while they talked of his adventures with the King, then Edward said:

'While I was away, I was always thinking of you. And now I have seen you again, I know that I must speak. I love you, Patience, and want to be with you always.'

Patience looked away. 'You saved my life, and I can never forget that, Edward,' she said quietly. 'I know that you're my friend, and I thank you for your kind words. But I'm young and I must talk to my father.'

Edward did not understand her answer. What did she mean? Did she love him, or didn't she?

'Do you think that your father will say no because I'm only a poor forester?' he began.

Just then Mr Hetherstone came out into the garden

and called to them. 'Edward, I was looking for you. A letter has just arrived from Parliament. Look.'

The letter said that Parliament was giving Arnwood and its land to Mr Hetherstone. Edward's face turned white and for a minute he could not speak.

'We'll ride across tomorrow and look at Arnwood. I want to rebuild the house,' said Mr Hetherstone.

'But Arnwood belongs to the Beverley family,' Edward said carefully. 'Perhaps not all the children died in the fire. And if some of them are still alive . . .'

'I'll give Arnwood back, of course. But for now Arnwood belongs to me, and when Patience marries, it will belong to her husband.'

Edward was silent. He could not tell Mr Hetherstone his secret now, or that he wanted to marry his daughter.

That night he went to bed early, but could not sleep. 'Patience is rich now,' he thought, 'and many men will

For a minute Edward could not speak.

want to marry her. And I don't think that she loves me. And if I say I am Edward Beverley, I'm sure that Parliament will take Arnwood back, and I'll still be a poor forester. I can't stay here any more. I shall leave England, and go to the King in France.'

Very early the next morning, while everyone was still asleep, Edward left the house and rode across the forest to the cottage. There he made plans with Humphrey and his sisters. They were very sorry to see him so unhappy.

'It's time for Alice and Edith to leave the forest too,' Edward told Humphrey. 'While I was in the north with the King, I met the Conynghame family, who knew our father very well. They will be happy to take the girls and

Very early the next morning, Edward rode across the forest to the cottage.

look after them. Our sisters will have a better life there. And you, Humphrey – why don't you come with me?'

'No,' said Humphrey. 'It will be good for the girls to get away, but it's better that I stay here. Pablo and I can look after the farm together. Also, I can watch and see what happens to Arnwood. One day you'll come back, and who knows what will happen then?'

Edward left that night, and Alice and Edith cried very much. It was an unhappy time for them all – the end of their life together in the forest. Edward left a letter for Mr Hetherstone. 'You have been very kind to me, and I thank you,' he wrote. But he wrote nothing to Patience.

When Mr Hetherstone got Edward's letter, he rode over at once to see Humphrey. He, too, was very unhappy.

'All my plans have gone wrong,' he told Humphrey. 'Edward has gone, and my daughter is very unhappy. I've known for a long time that you were the Beverley children. I wanted Patience to marry Edward. She loves him, but she wanted to talk to me first, because she thought that Edward was a poor man. And I asked Parliament for Arnwood because I wanted to rebuild the house and then give it to Edward. Will you help me, Humphrey, to rebuild the house? One day the King will come back to England, and Edward will come back too. I want Arnwood to be ready for him.'

Edward was away for nearly nine years, fighting with the French army in France and Holland and Spain. But in May 1660, after Cromwell died, Charles II came back to be King of England, and Edward Beverley was with him when he rode into London.

The happiest day of all was when the children were together again at last.

Those were happy times in London. But the happiest day of all was the day when the Beverley children of the New Forest were together again at last.

'The farm at our cottage is now very large,' Humphrey told Edward. 'Mr Hetherstone rebuilt Arnwood and says that it belongs to you. He'll be happy to see you again.'

'And what about Patience?' Alice asked. 'Do you still love her, Edward? She's here in London, you know.'

'Yes, I saw her one day in the crowds at the King's house,' said Edward. 'She's more beautiful than ever. I still love her, but I'm sure that she has forgotten me.'

'You were very unkind to her,' Edith said. 'She was very unhappy when you went away. But she hasn't married anyone in these nine years, and lots of men have asked her. So I think that she still loves you.'

Edith was right, and about a year later Edward married Patience and they lived happily together at Arnwood. Oswald Partridge came to work for Edward there. Humphrey married the daughter of a friend, bought a bigger farm, and gave Jacob Armitage's cottage to Pablo. And Alice and Edith, now beautiful young women, married soldiers of the King. And there we will say goodbye to the Beverleys.

GLOSSARY

brave not afraid, showing no fear

bury to put a dead person in the ground

clean *(v)* to take away the dirt from something

farm land and buildings where people grow things to eat and keep animals for food

frighten to fill with fear, to make someone afraid

gipsy a person who travels a lot and does not make a home in one place

hate to dislike someone very much; opposite of 'to love'

hunt to catch and kill wild animals for food

king the most important man in a country

kiss to touch with the lips to show love

land *(n)* a piece of ground (e.g. gardens or a farm that belong to a house)

lift to take something or someone up

look after to take care of someone or something

oatmeal a kind of flour made from oats, used for food

Parliament the group of people who make the laws for a country

Parliamentary belonging to Parliament

pretend to do or be something which looks true but is not

rebuild to build again

Roundhead a person who fought for Parliament against the King in the seventeenth century

save to take someone or something out of danger

search to look very carefully when you want to find something

sir a polite word that you say when you speak to an older or a more important man

The Children of the New Forest

ACTIVITIES

Before Reading

1 Read the story introduction on the first page of the book and the back cover. How much do you know now about the story? Complete the sentences with the right names.

Cromwell / the children / Jacob / the King

1 _____ is in prison.
2 _____'s men have burnt _____'s home.
3 _____ escaped and are hiding in the New Forest.
4 _____'s father fought for _____ and was killed.
5 In 1647 it was dangerous to be a friend of _____.
6 _____ is _____'s one true friend.
7 With _____'s help, _____ learn to live off the land.

2 What is going to happen in the story? Can you guess? Tick one box for each sentence.

	YES	NO
1 King Charles is killed.	☐	☐
2 Cromwell's men find the Beverley children.	☐	☐
3 The Beverley children are always hungry.	☐	☐
4 Jacob Armitage dies.	☐	☐
5 Edward Beverley saves somebody's life.	☐	☐
6 Edward Beverley goes to fight for Cromwell.	☐	☐

While Reading

Read Chapter 1, and answer these questions.

Why

1 . . . were the soldiers planning to burn Arnwood?

2 . . . did Jacob visit the children every day?

3 . . . did Edward agree to leave Arnwood?

4 . . . did Edward want to fight Cromwell's soldiers?

5 . . . was cooking and cleaning new work to the children?

6 . . . did the soldiers search Jacob's cottage?

7 . . . did Jacob tell the children to pretend to be ill?

8 . . . did Jacob and the children have to cook two dinners?

Read Chapter 2, then complete these sentences with the right names.

1 _____ bought cottage clothes for the children to wear.

2 _____ learned to read and write.

3 _____ learned how to mend clothes.

4 _____ shot his first deer in May.

5 _____ sold some deer meat and bought a little cart.

6 _____ had to learn how to pull the cart behind him.

7 _____ loved the work on the farm.

8 _____ drove the cow away from her calf.

Read Chapter 3. Here are some untrue sentences about it. Change them into true sentences.

1 Alice was ill that winter and could not leave the cottage.
2 Humphrey needed a dog to help with the hunting.
3 Edward told Mr Hetherstone his name was Beverley.
4 Mr Hetherstone was one of the King's good friends.
5 Mr Hetherstone thought the burning of Arnwood was a good thing.
6 Oswald Partridge did not give Edward one of his puppies.
7 Mr Hetherstone saved Patience from the fire.
8 Edward wanted Mr Hetherstone's thanks.

Read Chapter 4. Who said this, and to whom? Who or what were they talking about?

1 'We think he's dying.'
2 'In London he tried to stop the murder.'
3 'One day I shall fight against his murderers.'
4 'Well, this is happy news!'
5 'He cannot save you from the soldiers if they catch you killing the forest deer.'
6 'He never listened to Parliament.'
7 'I will pay you and you can help your family.'
8 'We shall all be friends.'
9 'I think the time is right for you to ride north and meet him.'

Before you read Chapter 5, can you guess what happens? Choose the best ending for these sentences.

1 Edward goes to fight for the King . . .
   a) and is killed.   b) and comes home safely.
2 Patience loves Edward . . .
   a) and she marries him.   b) but she doesn't marry him.
3 Mr Hetherstone knows that Edward is a Beverley . . .
   a) but he tells no one.   b) and he tells Cromwell's men.
4 The Beverley children go to live in different places . . .
   a) and never meet again.   b) and meet again in London.
5 King Charles II rides into London . . .
   a) many years later.   b) soon after Edward meets him.

Read Chapter 5, and join these halves of sentences.

1 Many of the King's soldiers were killed, . . .
2 Edward told Patience that he loved her, . . .
3 Parliament gave Arnwood to Mr Hetherstone, . . .
4 Edward couldn't ask Patience to marry him . . .
5 Humphrey stayed at the farm with Pablo, . . .
6 Patience had to wait for nine years . . .

7 but he did not understand her answer.
8 so he left England and went away to France.
9 before Edward came home and married her.
10 and Edward had to return secretly to the New Forest.
11 but his sisters went to live with friends in the north.
12 who planned to rebuild it and give it back to Edward.

After Reading

1 Find these 15 words in the word search, and draw lines through them. The words go from left to right, and from top to bottom.

bucket, burn, climb, cottage, farm, flames, forest, ladder, land, pot, pretend, save, search, smoke, stables

R	P	O	T	E	M	S	M	O	K	E	P	E
S	M	L	A	D	D	E	R	B	F	E	R	C
T	R	F	Y	C	L	I	M	B	L	O	E	O
A	U	O	A	F	A	R	M	R	A	E	T	T
B	U	R	N	M	N	Y	G	R	M	A	E	T
L	N	E	D	C	D	S	A	V	E	H	N	A
E	I	S	S	E	A	R	C	H	S	L	D	G
S	D	T	R	E	B	U	C	K	E	T	N	E

Now write down all the letters that don't have a line through them. Begin with the first line and go across each line to the end. You will have 29 letters, which will make a sentence of 5 words.

1 What is the sentence, who said it, and to whom?
2 Was it true?
3 Why did the person say it?

2 All these words come from the story. Put them into three groups, under these headings.

| ANIMALS | FOOD | FIGHTING |

army	cow	gun	pig	soldier
bread	deer	horse	potatoes	sword
calf	eggs	meat	puppy	uniform
chickens	enemy	milk	salt	vegetables

3 Use the words below, and some of the words from your three lists above, to complete this passage.

making, caught, cleaned, cook, cooked, fight, fighting,
hunt, planted, rode, worked

The children all _____ hard. Every spring they _____ lots
of different _____ in the fields. Alice _____ the house and
learned how to _____, and Edith made oatmeal _____ and
_____ it on the stones by the fire. She also looked after the
_____ and went to get the _____ every morning.

Humphrey was clever at _____ things out of wood. One
day he _____ a wild _____ and her new-born _____ in the
forest, so then they had _____ to drink.

Edward learned to _____ the red _____ of the forest, but
he always wanted to be a _____. One day he _____ away,
with his father's _____ by his side, to _____ for the King.
He came home wearing a dead Roundhead's _____. After
that he was away for years, _____ with the French _____.

4 Here is a new illustration for the story. Find the best place in the story to put the picture, and answer these questions.

The picture goes on page ____.

1 Who are the people in this picture?
2 What has just happened in the story?
3 What happens next?

Now write a caption for the illustration.

Caption: _____

5 **What did Mr Hetherstone say to Patience when he got Edward's letter? Put their conversation in the right order and write in the speakers' names. Mr Hetherstone speaks first (number 3).**

1 _____ 'I hope we will, child. I hope he'll be your husband one day. You love him, don't you?'

2 _____ 'Beverley? You mean the Beverleys of Arnwood?'

3 _____ 'Patience, I've just had a letter from Edward.'

4 _____ 'Oh Father, why didn't you tell him that? Now he's gone to France, and it's too late . . .'

5 _____ 'He's gone to fight for the King in France.'

6 _____ 'Yes, I do, Father. But are you happy for me to marry a poor forester?'

7 _____ 'Yes. But all my plans have gone wrong. I wanted to rebuild Arnwood and give it back to him.'

8 _____ 'From Edward? Why? Where has he gone?'

9 _____ 'He isn't a forester. His name's Edward Beverley.'

10 _____ 'Oh no! Oh, Father, we'll never see him again.'

6 **What did you think about this story? Complete these sentences (you can use as many words as you want).**

1 I *liked / didn't like* _____ because _____.

2 _____ *was / were* lucky because _____.

3 I felt sorry for _____ when _____.

4 I felt angry with _____ when _____.

ABOUT THE AUTHOR

Frederick Marryat (usually known as Captain Marryat) was born in London in 1792, the son of a Member of Parliament. He always wanted to go to sea, and he joined the Royal Navy when he was only fourteen years old. During the war against Napoleon, he had many adventures at sea, and later he fought in the West Indies, in Burma, and against smugglers in the English Channel. He was a Commander by the time he was twenty-three, and in 1820 he was the captain of a ship which guarded Napoleon when the French emperor was in prison on the island of St Helena. Captain Marryat was also a very brave man, who saved the lives of many sailors.

In 1830 Marryat left the navy and became a writer. He wrote many novels about life at sea, but his best-known ones are *Peter Simple* (1834), and *Mr Midshipman Easy* (1836), which told the story of Jack Easy and his adventures in the navy. (A film was made of this story in 1935.) In later years Marryat, who had eleven children of his own, began writing stories for children. These included *Masterman Ready* (1841) and *The Children of the New Forest* (1847), which is his most famous book.

In 1843 Captain Marryat went to live on a farm in Norfolk. His daughter Florence, in her book about her father, wrote that he was a fine sea captain and a very good writer, but not very clever at farming. Marryat died in Norfolk in 1848, soon after the death at sea of his eldest son.

Captain Marryat is remembered today for his children's books. He had a very exciting life himself, and he knew how to make his adventure stories real and exciting for his readers.

OXFORD BOOKWORMS LIBRARY

Classics • Crime & Mystery • Factfiles • Fantasy & Horror
Human Interest • Playscripts • Thriller & Adventure
True Stories • World Stories

The OXFORD BOOKWORMS LIBRARY provides enjoyable reading in English, with a wide range of classic and modern fiction, non-fiction, and plays. It includes original and adapted texts in seven carefully graded language stages, which take learners from beginner to advanced level. An overview is given on the next pages.

All Stage 1 titles are available as audio recordings, as well as over eighty other titles from Starter to Stage 6. All Starters and many titles at Stages 1 to 4 are specially recommended for younger learners. Every Bookworm is illustrated, and Starters and Factfiles have full-colour illustrations.

The OXFORD BOOKWORMS LIBRARY also offers extensive support. Each book contains an introduction to the story, notes about the author, a glossary, and activities. Additional resources include tests and worksheets, and answers for these and for the activities in the books. There is advice on running a class library, using audio recordings, and the many ways of using Oxford Bookworms in reading programmes. Resource materials are available on the website <www.oup.com/bookworms>.

The *Oxford Bookworms Collection* is a series for advanced learners. It consists of volumes of short stories by well-known authors, both classic and modern. Texts are not abridged or adapted in any way, but carefully selected to be accessible to the advanced student.

You can find details and a full list of titles in the *Oxford Bookworms Library Catalogue* and *Oxford English Language Teaching Catalogues*, and on the website <www.oup.com/bookworms>.

THE OXFORD BOOKWORMS LIBRARY
GRADING AND SAMPLE EXTRACTS

STARTER • 250 HEADWORDS

present simple – present continuous – imperative –
can/cannot, must – *going to* (future) – simple gerunds ...

Her phone is ringing – but where is it?

Sally gets out of bed and looks in her bag. No phone. She looks under the bed. No phone. Then she looks behind the door. There is her phone. Sally picks up her phone and answers it. *Sally's Phone*

STAGE 1 • 400 HEADWORDS

... past simple – coordination with *and*, *but*, *or* –
subordination with *before*, *after*, *when*, *because*, *so* ...

I knew him in Persia. He was a famous builder and I worked with him there. For a time I was his friend, but not for long. When he came to Paris, I came after him – I wanted to watch him. He was a very clever, very dangerous man. *The Phantom of the Opera*

STAGE 2 • 700 HEADWORDS

... present perfect – *will* (future) – *(don't) have to, must not, could* –
comparison of adjectives – simple *if* clauses – past continuous –
tag questions – *ask/tell* + infinitive ...

While I was writing these words in my diary, I decided what to do. I must try to escape. I shall try to get down the wall outside. The window is high above the ground, but I have to try. I shall take some of the gold with me – if I escape, perhaps it will be helpful later. *Dracula*

... should, may – present perfect continuous – *used to* – past perfect –
causative – relative clauses – indirect statements ...

Of course, it was most important that no one should see
Colin, Mary, or Dickon entering the secret garden. So Colin
gave orders to the gardeners that they must all keep away
from that part of the garden in future. *The Secret Garden*

STAGE 4 • 1400 HEADWORDS

... past perfect continuous – passive (simple forms) –
would conditional clauses – indirect questions –
relatives with *where/when* – gerunds after prepositions/phrases ...

I was glad. Now Hyde could not show his face to the world
again. If he did, every honest man in London would be proud
to report him to the police. *Dr Jekyll and Mr Hyde*

STAGE 5 • 1800 HEADWORDS

... future continuous – future perfect –
passive (modals, continuous forms) –
would have conditional clauses – modals + perfect infinitive ...

If he had spoken Estella's name, I would have hit him. I was so
angry with him, and so depressed about my future, that I could
not eat the breakfast. Instead I went straight to the old house.
Great Expectations

STAGE 6 • 2500 HEADWORDS

... passive (infinitives, gerunds) – advanced modal meanings –
clauses of concession, condition

When I stepped up to the piano, I was confident. It was as if I
knew that the prodigy side of me really did exist. And when I
started to play, I was so caught up in how lovely I looked that
I didn't worry how I would sound. *The Joy Luck Club*

BOOKWORMS • HUMAN INTEREST • STAGE 2

Anne of Green Gables

L. M. MONTGOMERY

Retold by Clare West

Marilla Cuthbert and her brother Matthew want to adopt an orphan, to help on the farm at Green Gables. They ask for a boy, but they get Anne, who has red hair and freckles, and who talks and talks and talks.

They didn't want a girl, but how can they send a child back, like an unwanted parcel? So Anne stays, and begins a new life in the sleepy, quiet village of Avonlea in Canada.

But it is not so quiet after Anne comes to live there . . .

BOOKWORMS • CLASSICS • STAGE 2

Robinson Crusoe

DANIEL DEFOE

Retold by Diane Mowat

'I often walked along the shore, and one day I saw something in the sand. I went over to look at it more carefully . . . It was a footprint – the footprint of a man!'

In 1659 Robinson Crusoe was shipwrecked on a small island off the coast of South America. After fifteen years alone, he suddenly learns that there is another person on the island. But will this man be a friend – or an enemy?